Where Kids Go to School Around the World

ALBATROS

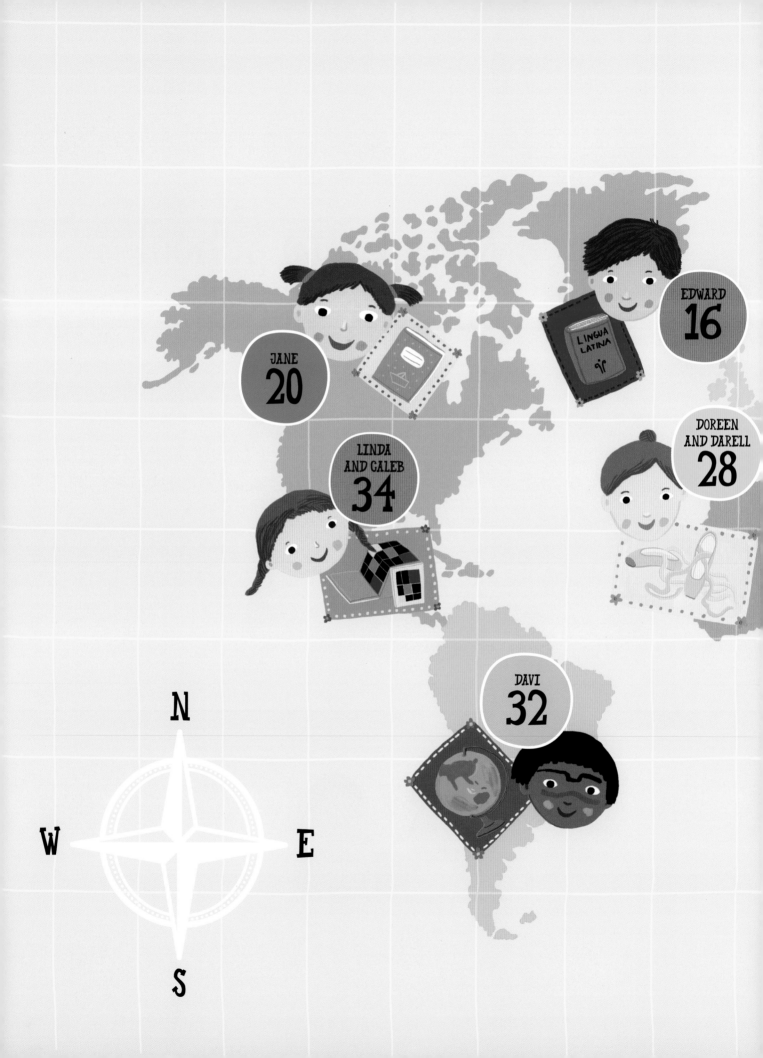

Yay! We're off to school!

Maybe you already go to school. Or maybe you haven't started quite yet. Imagine all the places where children like you grab their books and make their way to school every day! Whether it's a big city, a tiny village, a desert, a rainforest, or somewhere down by the sea or up in the mountains, there's a school there. Children are the same everywhere, but are schools the same? Far from it! What students learn in class and how they acquire new knowledge depends on the country they live in and its culture. The differences are huge!

I like going to school!

My favorite subject is gymnastics!

They don't give us grades at Montessori school!

My school is high in the mountains.

Animals make me feel happy.

Do all children go to school?

It used to be the norm that children from poorer families didn't go to school. Instead, they began working at a very young age to help support the family. It was common for boys to be educated in reading, writing, and math, but not girls. In some countries, this is sadly still the case. But everyone on Earth has the right to an education! Today, international organizations work to ensure that all children—regardless of gender, age, ethnicity, nationality, or faith—can go to school. And year after year, more and more kids are going to school. Even so, every twelfth child in the world is still unable to go to school.

I have lots of friends at school!

Does age matter?

The age at which children start school is not the same in every country. In England and Argentina, for instance, schooling is compulsory from age 4, while Finnish and Indonesian children don't start school until they are 7. But have no fear: good teachers are prepared to teach students large and small.

My parents are proud of me!

School on a boat in Bangladesh

HI! MY NAME'S **ANIKA**, AND I COME FROM **BANGLADESH**. AS OUR VILLAGE IS IN A REGION CUT OFF FROM THE REST OF THE WORLD BY THE MONSOON FOR MUCH OF THE YEAR, I CAN'T GO TO SCHOOL. SO GUESS WHAT? A FLOATING SCHOOL COMES TO ME! THANKS TO SCHOOLS ON BOATS, MY FRIENDS AND I GET AN EDUCATION ALL YEAR ROUND.

10 Life affected by floods

In the past, the children of our village were unable to go to school during the floods—because the water stopped them from reaching the city, where the school was located. Sadly, due to the global climate emergency, the monsoon where we live is an ever-greater problem that causes devastating flooding.

1 A boat that is both old and new

Our school is made out of a traditional local kind of boat called a nauka. It is 50 feet long and 10 feet wide, and its roof—reinforced with metal beams—can withstand the heaviest rain. We are perfectly safe in our floating school.

2 Energy from the sun

Our boat takes its electricity from solar panels on its roof. This allows us to work with computers and an internet connection. How lucky we are: ours are the only computers in the village!

3 Learning at any time of day

So that we can revise our schoolwork in the evenings at home, each of us has a small solar-powered lamp—a brilliant invention. I love to read when my younger brothers and sisters are asleep, and our home is quiet.

4 The library on the boat

Our classroom has a library from which we can borrow all kinds of books whenever we wish.

বিদ্যালয়

9 The boat as a school bus

Every morning, our floating school picks up children at a number of coastal stops. It takes us all home again in the afternoon.

8 Sustainability and thrift

As we see for ourselves how the mishandling of nature affects human life, in class we spend a lot of time learning about environmental protection. My parents come to the school to attend courses on the safe fertilization of crops.

7 Schoolbooks for everyone

We get our textbooks, exercise books, and stationery for free. All parents support us in our education, believing that thanks to school we will not grow up to be poor.

6 Our ABCs are important, and so are other things

Thanks to our great teacher, we can already read and write in Bengali. We spend some time each day doing math, and we also learn practical skills, such as purifying contaminated water.

HELLO, MY NAME'S
ANIKA

5 Let's go to the play boat!

Lying at anchor next to our boat is another boat with a slide, swings, and climbing frames. Imagine that! We adore this waterborne playground, especially at break time!

School in Japan

HI! MY NAME'S **HITOMU**, AND I LIVE IN **JAPAN**, WHERE WE HOLD EDUCATION IN HIGH REGARD. JAPANESE SCHOOLS ARE KNOWN FOR BEING VERY DEMANDING AND FOR EMPHASIZING DOING WELL IN EXAMS. I SPEND A LOT OF TIME DOING HOMEWORK, EVEN ON HOLIDAYS, AND I HAVE DONE SO SINCE I WAS SMALL. BUT AS YOU'LL SEE, IT'S NOT ALL STRESS AT SCHOOL—WE HAVE LOTS OF FUN TOO!

10 It's up to us to keep things neat and tidy

We Japanese schoolchildren clean up after ourselves. We mop the floor, wipe down the desks, and clean the blackboard; we even wash the windows. This teaches us to respect our surroundings and not make unnecessary messes.

1 A respectful start to the day

We start the school day by standing to sing the school song together. After this, we bow to our teacher in a respectful greeting. When the day is over, we bow to the teacher again before we leave school.

2 Groups for all kinds of hobbies

After class, I don't go straight home, because I spend time in hobby groups organized by our school. In addition to all kinds of sports, we can choose from activities including *kendo* (traditional Japanese swordsmanship), *shodo* (calligraphy), *sado* (the Japanese tea ceremony), *ikebana* (flower-arranging), and *haiku* (short Japanese poems).

HELLO, MY NAME'S **HITOMU**

3 A uniform for a sense of togetherness

At our school, we wear a uniform. Some of my classmates don't like the uniform much, but no one complains. For us, togetherness and the greater good of the group are very important.

8

9 Earthquakes!

As earthquakes are common in Japan, at school we often do drills to prepare for such a disaster. In an earthquake, we crawl under the desk immediately, put on a special head-protecting cap, and hold onto the desk.

8 School starts at springtime

Our school year is divided into three terms. It begins in April, when the trees are in bloom. We welcome new students at a traditional ceremony, and we have another ceremony to mark the end of the school year.

7 Meshiagare!

This is our way of saying "Bon appétit." As the meal is served in the classroom, no one goes home for lunch. Children dressed in an apron and headscarf serve everyone with the same healthy food. No one would dream of having a hamburger and fries instead!

6 Randoseru

Before I started in the first grade, my parents bought me a *randoseru*, the traditional leather backpack in which we Japanese schoolchildren carry the books and stationery we use each day.

5 Three types of writing

To read and write in Japanese, we must learn three types of writing. *Higana* and *katakana* are syllabaries (sets of symbols representing syllables), while *kanji* is logographic (meaning it has characters for individual words).

4 Uwabaki

In Japan, we remove our shoes indoors. To make sure we don't bring mud into the classroom, as soon as we get to school, we change into special cloth slippers called *uwabaki*. Practical, aren't they?

School in Finland

MY NAME'S **TAINI**. I LIVE IN **FINLAND**, BEYOND THE ARCTIC CIRCLE. IN OUR RURAL AREA, THERE IS ONLY ONE SCHOOL, AND EVERYONE IN IT KNOWS EVERYONE ELSE. ALTHOUGH WE ARE A GOOD DISTANCE AWAY FROM THE NEAREST BIG CITY, OUR LIFE HERE IS ANYTHING BUT BACKWARD. YOU MAY BE SURPRISED TO LEARN HOW MODERN OUR SCHOOL IS INSIDE.

10 Kids should act like kids

We Finns don't start school until we are seven. Before then, we have plenty of time to enjoy childhood to the fullest. Even at school, play is understood as an excellent way to learn.

1 Well-being comes first

Our school is fitted and furnished with our comfort in mind. We can spend time at our desks, on a sofa, even on a favorite exercise ball. We are always happy to change our seating plan.

2 Local school curricula

In Finland, each school adapts the curriculum to their own needs. At our school, for instance, we sometimes talk about the Sámi people, the original inhabitants of northern Scandinavia.

3 A good night's sleep

Our classes don't start until 9:30 a.m., and we have only a few lessons each day. This gives us lots of time to relax and have fun. Plus, in the morning we can sleep in.

HELLO,
MY NAME'S
TAINI

4 The value of teamwork

As is common in Finland, our teacher places great importance on a friendly atmosphere and teamwork. After all, each of us has different talents. If we work together, we get the best results.

9 Technology in the modern world

At school, we often work with computers, tablets, and an interactive board. We learn computer programming and practice it with educational computer games. But don't be fooled. We don't spend all our time indoors. We go outside to learn from nature too.

8 Teachers are family friends

One teacher teaches us all subjects, all the way through sixth grade. As a result, they get to know us very well. In Finland, the teaching profession is highly regarded. Only the best students get a place at a teacher-training college. Finnish education is among the world's best, possibly because our teachers are so enthusiastic.

7 Long-distance school buses

In the Finnish countryside, people live quite far apart. A bus picks us up from even the most remote places—that way, we don't have to traipse through the woods or across snowy plains to get to school.

6 School for all

The school does its best to make everyone's learning easier. We get our schoolbooks and our lunch for free, and school psychologists are always around to help. Children who have limited Finnish because they were born abroad can attend special language classes.

5 No stressful tests

Many people think that because we are one of the world's best-educated nations our teachers must give us test after test. But the opposite is true! Besides, we are learning for our whole lives, not just for school.

School in the Himalayas

HI! MY NAME'S **GAURAV**. WELCOME TO OUR SCHOOL, WHICH IS SITUATED ON A SLOPE AMONG THE PEAKS OF THE **HIMALAYAS**, THE HIGHEST MOUNTAIN RANGE ON EARTH. OUR REGION IS VERY DIFFICULT TO GET TO. IN FACT, THERE IS NO ROAD LEADING TO IT. LIKE OUR NEIGHBORS, MY FAMILY CAN'T AFFORD TO PAY FOR ME TO GO TO SCHOOL IN TOWN, SO I'M VERY GRATEFUL FOR OUR SCHOOL IN THE MOUNTAINS. IT'S LIKE A MAGICAL GATEWAY TO THE WORLD!

10 We are all equal

Have you noticed our school uniform? We wear it with pride because we are proud of our school. Our parents spent their childhoods working, but we will change the world one day!

1 Daily hiking

My morning walk to school takes me over an hour. I have to descend to the valley, then follow narrow paths to the opposite hill. A group of us kids from the neighborhood all walk together, though, so it's fun.

2 Daily assemblies

The school day begins in front of the school, where we do exercises, sing the school's song, and say a prayer before one of us recites a poem. To be called on to speak in front of the others is a great honor, but can also be scary.

3 Teachers from all over the world

As well as teachers from the locality, the teaching staff of our school includes volunteers from abroad. They tell us in English about their culture, and they get to learn about life in the Himalayas. It's great fun, learning English in this way!

4 Latecomers are punished

Even though the school day doesn't begin until 10 o'clock, a student sometimes arrives late. Latecomers aren't allowed to join the morning assembly.

12

9 Modest, but with love

Our school might be built of corrugated iron, and we might not have the internet, but you won't find smarter teachers or better-motivated students anywhere!

8 Rare fruit

Thanks to school, every week we get a chance to eat fruit our families can't afford, such as bananas and apples. Yum!

7 Reading, writing, and arithmetic

As well as studying the local language, English, and mathematics, we spend a lot of time learning about the natural world around us and environmental protection. I love the singing, dancing, and acting we do in class!

HELLO, MY NAME'S **GAURAV**

6 Discipline is strict

We have great respect for our teachers. We always stand up before answering their questions, sitting down again only after the teacher asks us to. And if one of the volunteers forgets to ask? Well, we stand patiently and wait.

5 The importance of exercise

Although our school subjects do not include PE, we like to exercise whenever we can. At break time we play table tennis and baseball, and sometimes we have races. On your marks, get set, go!

School in a refugee camp

HI! MY NAME'S **MAYA**. A FEW YEARS AGO, MY WHOLE FAMILY AND I HAD TO FLEE FROM OUR HOMES BECAUSE OF THE WAR. NOW WE LIVE IN A LARGE **REFUGEE CAMP**.

9 Missing home

Although I have friends here and go to a school with great teachers, I still get homesick. Every day, I ask myself when we will be able to go back. Keep your fingers crossed for me that it will be soon.

1 Schools in the camp

Fortunately, there are several schools here at the refugee camp. As I'm a student at one of them, I get to read and learn from schoolbooks. For me, studying is great fun.

2 My beloved schoolbooks

We had to leave home in such a rush that my schoolbag with all my books got left behind in the chaos. I was very upset about this. I want to be a doctor someday, so I really need my schoolbooks.

HELLO, MY NAME'S **MAYA**

3 Girls in the morning, boys in the afternoon

As all schools at the camp are full to bursting, we have lessons in two groups. We girls go to school in the morning, while the boys go in the afternoon.

14

8 Art helps with stress

When you get caught up in a war and are forced to leave your home, you get sad—especially if you're still a kid. That's why there's a special program here at the camp called Heart. It helps us to deal with the traumas of war through dancing, drawing, and talking.

7 Full classrooms

Even so, all classrooms are full. On the one hand, this is great: you can make lots of new friends all at once. On the other hand, if anyone falls behind in their learning, it's harder for the teacher to help them catch up.

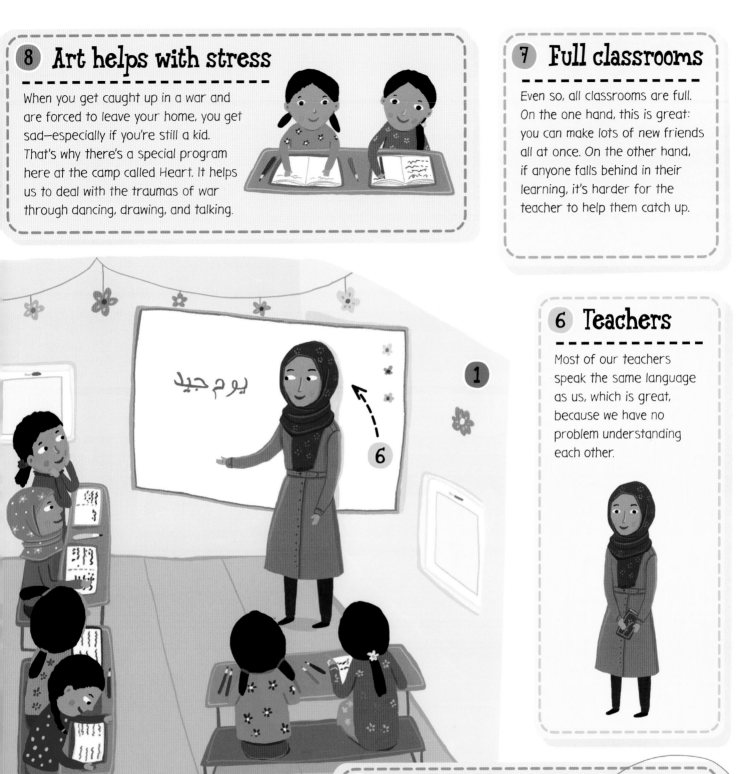

يوم جيد

6 Teachers

Most of our teachers speak the same language as us, which is great, because we have no problem understanding each other.

4 Concerned moms

Not all moms are willing to send their children to a camp school. This is not because they are against education but because they are afraid that something bad could happen to us on our way to school. Life in the camp can be pretty tough, but we do our best.

5 Sports at the camp

While we girls are doing our lessons, the boys are flexing their muscles in the schoolyard. They jump and run, but most of all they play soccer. We girls like all of these activities too, as well as skipping rope. Dodgeball is a new favorite of ours—although it hurts a lot when a friend takes you out!

Boarding school in England

HI! MY NAME'S **EDWARD**, AND I'M A STUDENT AT A PRIVATE BOARDING SCHOOL IN **ENGLAND**. AS BOARDERS, WE LIVE AT THE SCHOOL IN TERM TIME. ALTHOUGH YOU MAY BE HEARING ABOUT SUCH SCHOOLS FOR THE FIRST TIME, THEY HAVE A LONG TRADITION IN ENGLAND. MY FATHER, MOTHER, GRANDFATHER, AND GREAT-GRANDFATHER ATTENDED THE VERY SAME SCHOOL!

1 Future Ladies and Gentlemen

Some private boarding schools only take boys, as they have traditionally always done. Some take only girls. But in our school, both boys and girls study together.

2 Tradition above all

Our school is over 1,000 years old, so it has quite a history! We have our own uniform, motto, and song, as well as many strict rules, some of which are very old. Sometimes I feel like I live in a castle—which is great!

10 Lifelong friendship

As we spend all our time together, I know that I can always rely on my classmates. I believe that we will stay friends our whole lives long.

3 School order and culture

We may live away from our parents, but don't get to thinking that we bring ourselves up. Our teachers ensure that we adopt the ethics, values, and longstanding culture of our school. Many students have been expelled from our school for bad behavior. How shameful!

9 Latin is of prime importance

As well as regular subjects such as mathematics and English, we study Latin and Ancient Greek. Believe it or not, these classical languages are my favorite subjects!

8 Toughening the body

I don't spend all day over my books, you know. My schoolmates and I like to play baseball and football in the school grounds, and we ride horses and row in the nearby river.

HELLO, I AM
EDWARD

7 School fees

My parents pay high fees for our education. They are proud of us for passing the entrance examination and interview. They trust our teachers to prepare us for study at one of the world's best universities.

6 When we get homesick

Being at home only during the holidays can be hard. But I telephone my parents twice a week, so I know exactly what goes on at home, and they know that I am doing well. I love speaking with my parents.

4 Supervised by prefects

Younger students like me are supervised by prefects as well as teachers. Prefects are older students chosen to take care of us, but they can also issue punishments. Acts of violence and other bad behavior aren't tolerated.

5 Study hard and do your prep

We are expected to study hard every evening and prepare actively for class. My teachers are strict and demanding. We even have lessons on Saturday mornings!

School in Uganda

HI! MY NAME'S **RASHIDA**, AND I'M FROM **UGANDA**, A PLACE LUSH WITH MOUNTAINS, RIVERS, GLACIERS, WATERFALLS, VALLEYS, AND LAKES. OF ALL THE COUNTRIES ON THE CONTINENT OF AFRICA, WE HAVE THE MOST LAKES—INCLUDING LAKE VICTORIA, WHICH IS SO LARGE THAT IT LOOKS LIKE THE SEA.

1 Fetching water

Although we have great lakes, we suffer from a shortage of drinking water. I regularly walk for 30 minutes to a well, where I fill a container with water. I then drag this heavy vessel all the way home, where my thirsty family are eagerly waiting for it.

2 At school

I also take a small water container to school so I can quench my thirst at break time. Our school has only one classroom, and it is so crowded that we sit many to a desk. Some of us even have to sit on the floor. What we all have in common is a thirst for knowledge.

10 Holidays

Although I like school, I'd be lying if I said I didn't like the holidays too. Our main vacation, in December and January, is almost two months long; the other two vacations are both one month long. But don't get to thinking that the holidays are just for relaxing— Mom always finds plenty of work for me to do around the house.

3 Improvised study aids

Our teacher is clever enough to answer all our questions. Because Uganda is a developing nation with no money for study aids, our teacher makes them for us. He teaches us new words in English using homemade flashcards. Thanks to a special clock he has made, even first-graders can tell the time.

9 Entertainment for parents

Don't get to thinking that school is only about sitting at a desk learning new information. School is fun too! For instance, having practiced our village's ritual dance to perfection in class, we perform it for our parents. Some are moved to tears by it.

8 School sets you up for life

So what do we learn at school? In addition to reading, writing, and arithmetic, we improve our knowledge of our local language and learn to speak English fluently. We don't forget about subjects like religious studies, geography, and history, of course. History is my favorite!

7 I study hard

Our parents encourage us to go to school because they believe that education will give us the chance of a better life. Although the education itself is free, not every family can afford their child's uniform, exercise books, or the fee for the final exams.

6 Lifelong education

Not only children acquire new knowledge at school; so, too, does our teacher. Once in a while, he rides his bike to a big school in the city, where he and other teachers compare experiences and learn from each other. They do this so that they may pass on only the best to their students.

HELLO, MY NAME'S

RASHIDA

5 The teacher is an authority

We look up to our teacher, as do our parents. Our village holds regular meetings for all its adults, at which they address common problems. Where he can, the teacher is happy to offer advice.

4 Yay for schoolbooks!

They say that kids in America have so many books they can barely carry them, but I find that hard to imagine. When our teacher receives a large package of books from humanitarian aid, we have real cause for celebration!

School in a hospital

HI! MY NAME'S **JANE**, AND I'VE BEEN IN THE **HOSPITAL** FOR SEVERAL MONTHS. FORTUNATELY, MY TREATMENT IS GOING WELL, AND I'LL BE ABLE TO GO HOME SOON. IT'S A GREAT HELP THAT I CAN GO TO SCHOOL WHILE I'M IN THE HOSPITAL.

9 Tomorrow we're going on a trip

Kids like me—who have been in the hospital for a while and are now getting better—sometimes go to the park with our teachers. We even go on school trips. These trips are no more demanding than we can manage, of course.

1 Hospital classroom

Every day, I go to the classroom attached to our ward. The other patients in the class are my friends. Our classroom looks just like one in a proper school building. We have an interactive whiteboard, computers, and many other learning aids.

2 Our teachers

You can tell a hospital teacher by the distinctive name badge on their chest.

3 Mathematics, etc.

Here in the hospital, we study the same things as students in ordinary schools. We even take tests, which our teachers at the hospital send to the teachers at our school.

4 Yay for playtime!

Another great thing about hospital schooling is that we play as well as learn. Sometimes we play board games. At other times, our teacher supervises when we role-play doctors and patients. This is a gentle way of preparing us for upcoming examinations, as well as explaining to us how the body works and why we are ill.

8 Home lessons

In some cases, a patient is discharged from the hospital while their treatment is ongoing and before they are ready to go back to school. For this reason, hospitals arrange for them to have lessons at home. I'm looking forward to being with my healthy schoolmates soon.

7 Drawing as therapy

To take our mind off our illness and our homesickness, our teachers give art classes in which we make all kinds of things. Not only are these super fun, but they cheer us up too!

HELLO, MY NAME'S JANE

6 Animal-assisted therapy

Our teacher sometimes brings a cat into class. We cuddle and pet the cat, and she purrs contentedly. This, too, lifts our spirits. She is brought to us for a reason: her presence really helps us. Treatment using cats is called "felinotherapy."

5 Learning in bed

Children whose health doesn't allow them to go to the hospital classroom are visited in their room by the teacher. It was like this for me too, in the beginning.

21

Buddhist monastic school

HI! MY NAME'S **JAMPA**. WELCOME TO OUR BUDDHIST MONASTIC SCHOOL IN **LADAKH**, INDIA! IF YOU WANTED TO VISIT ME, YOU WOULD HAVE TO CLIMB TO OVER TWO MILES ABOVE SEA LEVEL, TO THE HEART OF THE HIMALAYAS. HERE YOU WOULD FIND MY MONASTERY.

10 No desks

Our spacious classrooms contain no modern equipment. We sit on the floor, and the teacher walks among us. Classrooms don't even have electric outlets. And why should they, when there is no electricity before the evening?

1 I'm going to be a monk

A middle child, I was sent to the monastery by my parents. It was they who decided I would be a monk, and I respect their wishes. This makes it easier for me to accept that I may call home only once a month and visit my parents twice a year at most. Those who are forced to take this path find separation from home hard to bear.

2 Buddhism

As we will one day be monks, Buddhism provides the main content of our schooling. We learn to contemplate subjects such as compassion and the emptiness of all phenomena by debating them. In these debates, we defend our views in front of others.

3 Buddha

The religion of Buddhism was founded in the 5th century BCE by a wealthy prince named Siddhartha Gautama, who spent his youth in captivity at a palace, away from human suffering. Even so, Siddhartha witnessed ageing, illness, and death. As a result, he ran away from the palace to search for deliverance from suffering. After searching for six years, he achieved great insight, thus becoming the Enlightened One—aka, the Buddha.

9 Classroom or bedroom?

The room in which we sleep is also our classroom. As soon as we get up—at five-thirty in the morning—we must convert the bedroom into the classroom. After that, having washed in cold water, we are ready to pray.

8 Reciting mantras

We don't just play cricket! In the evening, we follow a period of self-study with the reciting of mantras and other Buddhist teachings under the supervision of a senior spiritual teacher from the monastery. Before we go to bed, we conduct philosophical disputations in pairs.

7 Cricket

Our lessons end at the stroke of four in the afternoon. Then it's time for some fun. Like all boys, we enjoy a bit of roughhousing. Most often we play cricket, our favorite game. I've had so much practice with the bat that I've become a player to be feared.

6 The school day

Every day, school starts at ten in the morning and continues for five hours. We pray together at six a.m. before having a hearty breakfast to ensure that we won't tire during our lessons. And what do we eat for breakfast? You can forget yogurt and cereal—our early-morning feast consists of lentils and vegetables, with Tibetan bread. Yum!

HELLO, MY NAME'S **JAMPA**

4 A monk's robes

My schoolmates and I wear scarlet robes, and our heads are shaved. Care of one's hair is a distraction from spiritual matters. Future monks should avoid such distractions.

5 What we study

Don't get to thinking that everything at our school revolves around religion. We also study mathematics, English, Tibetan, Hindi, and philosophy. Our school has several computers and a printer, allowing us to learn about information technology.

Sports school

HI! MY NAME'S **DANIELA**. I BET YOU'RE WONDERING WHERE I'VE BROUGHT YOU. WELL, YOU'RE IN THE LARGE GYMNASIUM AT MY SPORTS SCHOOL. WHEN I GROW UP, I WANT TO BE A PROFESSIONAL ATHLETE, LIKE MY DAD.

1 PE, then more PE

If you were to ask me about my favorite subject, naturally I'd tell you it's physical education, or "PE." And we do have an awful lot of it! We younger students have three PE classes a week. Older students have five. After our classes, we have afternoon training, of course.

2 Teacher and coach in one

Our classroom teacher is also a great sports coach. An hour ago, she was explaining our multiplication tables to us. Now she is showing us the basics of good running. If we master the right techniques, our performance will get better and better.

3 Warm-ups are crucial

It is important to warm up properly before each training session, race, competition, or match. A warm-up stretches the muscles and prepares you to do your best.

10 Competitions and medals

All our efforts in training are focused on competition in particular sports, where we compare our performance against other athletes of our own age. How I would love to win a gold medal this year!

4 Ready, set, go!

A good start is crucial. Sprinters push off in a crouching position from a starting block; this allows them to hit the track at lightning speed. Guided by our coach, we crouch and push off from the blocks until we get it right.

9 Spikes

To make our sprints over short distances as fast as possible, we wear special shoes with spikes on the soles.

8 Sports physicians

To guard against problems with our bodies and to show what they are best at, we go to see a sports physician once a year. This visit is fun: for instance, we get to use an exercise bike while the doctor measures our pulse rate.

HELLO, MY NAME'S **DANIELA**

7 Strong, flexible bodies

Even though we are future athletes, gymnastics and weights are an important part of our training. We do lots of leapfrogs, chin-ups, tumbles, and sit-ups, and we exercise with dumbbells.

6 Disciplines

At first, we get to know all disciplines of athletics, to find out which we are best suited to. We learn about techniques of the high jump, throwing the javelin, and hurdling. In the long jump, it's important to get your run-up right and not overstep the mark.

5 Swimming

Instruction in athletics includes regular swimming lessons. At first, I wasn't great in the water, but with time I've improved. Now I can do all of the swimming strokes.

A Muslim girls school

HI! MY NAME'S **MANELI**, AND I'M **MUSLIM**. EIGHT O'CLOCK IS APPROACHING, SO MY SCHOOL DAY IS ABOUT TO BEGIN. I'M LUCKY ENOUGH TO ATTEND A MUSLIM SCHOOL FOR GIRLS. QUIET NOW—OUR TEACHER IS ENTERING THE CLASSROOM.

1 The Koran

The Koran is the most important text of the Islamic religion. We believe that it is a message from Allah and that its 114 chapters (known as suras) were dictated to Muhammad (the founder of Islam) by the Archangel Gabriel in the 7th century CE.

2 What we learn

As well as reading, writing, and arithmetic, we have PE, art, and practical skills classes. Religion is a very important subject. We learn to interpret the Koran, and we study Persian literature.

3 Girls in uniform

Every girl in the class wears a uniform, and I think we look good in it. Students at boys schools wear a uniform only if their school requires them to.

10 Chador

The traditional clothing is a long, flowing robe called a chador, which covers us from head to toe. Our only other option is a headscarf and a long blouse. Either way, our heads are covered.

HELLO, MY NAME'S **MANELI**

4 A big fat zero

Our teacher scores our achievements on a scale of 0–20. That's right—a very badly prepared student gets a 0, which goes down badly with parents. But students who score a 20 are in for a family party!

9 Covered hair

We girls, like our teacher, cover our hair to signal pride in our religion. Sadly, in some countries, girls are punished for uncovered hair. Usually we have the option and I prefer to wear the hijab to signal pride in my culture.

8 Yay for lunchtime!

As classes end at noon, there are no canteens at our schools. We go home for lunch. It is common for the mother to stay at home to care full-time for the family until the children finish school.

7 Six days a week

The school day starts at eight a.m. and ends at noon. Afternoon classes are voluntary and mainly for exam preparation. We go to school six days a week. My favorite day is Friday because it's our day off.

5 Healthy body, healthy mind

The school day always starts at eight. After our teacher enters the classroom, we do a few stretching exercises to warm up, thus putting us in the right frame of mind for learning. After our exercises and before our lessons, we sing the school song.

6 Tests and exams

Oh dear—it's test time. At some point in the school year, our teacher calls us up to the board for an oral examination. And at the end of each semester, we take comprehensive written exams in all subjects. To prepare for these exams, we are given just one day's leave from our studies.

Ballet school

HI! WE'RE **DOREEN** AND **DARELL**, AND WE ARE TWINS. WE LIVE IN LONDON, WHERE WE GO TO BALLET SCHOOL. WE'VE LOVED MOVING ALONG WITH MUSIC SINCE WE WERE SMALL. OUR PARENTS HAD NO PROBLEM DECIDING WHICH SCHOOL TO SEND US TO!

10 Music

Every dance hall in the world has a piano in one corner. We exercise and train to the sound of music. Dance without music is unthinkable.

1 Dance hall

Our classroom is a spacious dance hall with an enormous mirror and poles. Here we spend hour after hour, working very, very hard. We look in the mirror to make sure that we are performing our moves as we should.

2 Pointes-ow!

The uncomfortable ballet shoes with reinforced toes and hard soles are known as pointes. As the name suggests, dancers wear them to move about gracefully on their tiptoes. Gracefully, yes—but in practice every movement in these shoes hurts SO MUCH! Boy dancers are lucky that they don't have to wear them.

3 Jumping and spinning

We boys spend day after day learning to jump in the dance hall. Every proper professional dancer must be able to make flawless, graceful jumps. The girls must work hard on their pirouettes. The mere sight of that makes my head spin!

4 We study hard too

Don't get to thinking that ballet school is only about dancing. We hit the books for mathematics, history, science, and other subjects too. But while students elsewhere have free time after school, we spend our afternoons dancing and training.

9 Stretching and more stretching

Dancers—girls and boys—must be extremely flexible. As well as strengthening our bodies by jumping, we are constantly supervised by instructors as we stretch and bend our limbs in search of perfection.

8 Basic ballet positions

Classical dance is based on five positions, which all of us must master. Our teachers go from one student to the next, checking our progress and correcting mistakes.

HELLO,
WE ARE
DOREEN
AND DARELL

7 Teachers

Our instructors tend to be former professional dancers who used to perform in world-famous theatrical productions. They do their best to pass on their experiences to us beginners. I hope that my brother and I will one day get the chance to dance on the best stages. But there's a lot of hard work ahead of us before that can happen.

6 Ballet slippers

We all wear special ballet slippers. Their soft uppers and thin soles adjust to every movement of the foot.

5 Sweatpants and booties

We go straight from the dance hall to the classroom. At our lessons, we wear sweatpants or a jumpsuit, because we must keep our legs warm at all times. Instead of slippers, we wear warm booties.

Australian 'School of the Air'

HI! MY NAME'S **LUKE**. MY PARENTS OWN A FARM IN THE **AUSTRALIAN** OUTBACK. WE LIVE CUT OFF FROM CIVILIZATION, SURROUNDED BY RED SOIL, KANGAROOS, AND OSTRICHES. WE ARE 200 MILES FROM THE NEAREST HARD-SURFACE ROAD AND 600 MILES FROM A SCHOOL. PRETTY AMAZING, ISN'T IT?

9 Physical education

Our teacher ends each school day with a period of exercise. We skip and do stretches together. The fact remains, however, that I run more on the farm and in the bush than I ever would in a gym.

1 Modern technology

As the nearest school is so far away, I walk to school every day. To be clear, my classroom is actually my bedroom. At eight o'clock, I sit down at my desk, switch on my computer, and log on with my teacher. My classmates live on remote farms too.

2 Before the school day starts

I get up around six a.m. Before the school day, I have my breakfast, then help my parents on the farm. One of my jobs is to feed the chickens.

3 Airplane deliveries

Wow, an airplane! Every two weeks, a plane flies to the bush with packages for me, containing workbooks from my teacher. I complete the exercises and return the books to him—also by plane.

4 Off to school-yay!

Once a year, we students meet up at the school building in the city for our compulsory sports day. It's great to do sport and chat together.

30

8 Support from parents

My parents sometimes help me with my homework, of course—especially when I don't know what to do or when the task is too difficult for me to manage on my own.

7 Picture this!

Our teacher sits in a TV studio in front of a board, where he writes and draws things we need to know about. Through the camera lens, the teacher also shows us teaching models and natural history aids.

6 Teacher's visit

From time to time, our teacher gets into an off-road vehicle and drives out to see each of his students on the farm. He spends two days with each, answering all of the students questions. I always look forward to a visit from my teacher!

5 Radio days

In the 1960s, my grandmother went to a distance-learning school, as I do now. In those days, however, there were no computers, so the teacher gave lessons by radio communication.

HELLO, MY NAME'S **LUKE**

School in the rainforest

HI! MY NAME'S **DAVI**, AND I LIVE WITH MY FAMILY IN THE **AMAZON RAINFOREST**. WE BELONG TO THE YANOMAMI TRIBE. AS WE CHOOSE TO SHUN THE MODERN WORLD, I DON'T GO TO SCHOOL AS YOU WOULD UNDERSTAND IT. FROM MY PARENTS AND THE WISEST MEMBERS OF OUR TRIBE, I GRADUALLY LEARN EVERYTHING I WILL NEED TO KNOW WHEN I'M A GROWN-UP.

9 Manual work is a must

This is where I learn basket-weaving. In the next room, I learn how to make pots. I don't attend any courses; I just watch the adults at work and imitate what I see.

1 Conservation of nature comes first

Our traditional way of life is founded on the conservation of nature. This is obvious—without nature, we wouldn't survive! Just yesterday, my dad and I planted new trees, which we will tend.

2 Telephone in a hut

In our village, no one has a mobile telephone. When a stranger visits, we kids like to borrow his phone to look at pictures and listen to music. But I can't understand how some city children spend all day on this thing. I would die of boredom!

3 A perfect understanding of the rainforest

Basic abilities necessary for survival in the rainforest include recognizing poisonous plants, using medicinal plants, and finding edible berries, leaves, and roots. We have a perfect understanding of the rainforest—better than that of many urban scientists.

SÓLIDO TÜKAGULINHÜ
LÍQUIDO HUA
GASOSO ÉITITSE
hëtmari

8 Messing around with friends

Even after a hard day, I always find time to play in the river with my friends!

7 Tradition and the modern world

Another thing I learn from my elders is the spiritual significance of skin-painting. Although we usually wear T-shirts and shorts, we have lots of fun painting our tribe's traditional red and black lines on our bodies!

6 The most important thing

Our will to hold on to our traditional way of life is also connected with our faith. We believe that every living being, thing, and place has its spirit. When strangers harm nature—by felling trees, for example—they also damage its spirits. Do they not know that they are endangering not just our culture but life on Earth itself?

5 What about my ABCs?

Some of our tribe's villages have schoolrooms. Here, children learn arithmetic as well as how to read and write in our native language and Portuguese. We all hope that this learning will enable us to defend the rights of indigenous peoples in the modern world.

HELLO, MY NAME'S DAVI

4 How to succeed in the hunt

The men take us boys with them on the hunt: seeing hunters' tactics for ourselves is far more practical than reading about them in books. We also learn to leave no traces in the forest.

Montessori school

HI! MY NAME'S **CALEB**. MY YOUNGER SISTER **LINDA** AND I ARE GETTING READY FOR SCHOOL. WE'RE REALLY LOOKING FORWARD TO IT! OUR SCHOOL IS SO MUCH FUN. NO BORING INFORMATION DRILLS HERE. IF YOU DON'T BELIEVE ME, TAKE A LOOK IN OUR **MONTESSORI** CLASSROOM.

1 Age doesn't matter

Although I'm two years older than Linda, we are in the same class. That's because children of different ages learn together at Montessori schools, with the older helping the younger.

2 Teacher as counselor

As she supervises our independent work, our teacher is always on hand to offer help and advice. It is important to her that we feel as secure as possible at school.

3 Where are the desks?

In our classroom, we sit not at desks but in a circle on the floor, on comfortable cushions—which suits everyone. It is very important that we should all feel comfortable.

10 Other alternative schools

Montessori schools aren't the only alternative schools. Our city also has a Dalton school, which highlights the individuality of the learner, and where students work on interesting presentations and projects. At Waldorf schools, students follow the lead of the teacher, whom they take as a role model.

HELLO, WE ARE **LINDA** AND **CALEB**

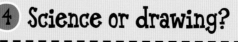

4 Science or drawing?

I'm reading an encyclopedia about interesting animals. Linda feels like drawing, so that's what she's doing. Two other classmates are looking at a map. This is another way in which our school is different: we each choose the subject we are in the mood to study.

9 No school bags

Take a look around. Bags filled with schoolbooks are nowhere to be seen. We bring nothing to school but a snack. All the learning materials we use remain in the classroom, so we go home empty-handed.

8 Montessori aids

One of the principles of Montessori schooling is that things should be handled so that as many senses as possible are involved. This explains why the learning aids in our classrooms are pretty unique. They include cards with numbers and letters, wooden squares to represent hundreds and thousands, and various folding tools. These aids help us find answers without having to ask the teacher.

7 No grades

Our teacher never gives grades. She talks things through with us, then gives us a verbal evaluation. Verbal evaluations also feature on our end-of-term certificates.

6 Nature as teacher

Our teachers know that nature is the best teacher. We regularly go for an all-day walk—to study interesting insects and plants, for instance. We also bring stones to class, where we talk about them, look them up in encyclopedias, and find out their names.

5 Respect for others

Our teacher makes sure that we learn to respect others. We learn that each of us is unique, and that we students set the rules by which we live together. If we get into an argument, our teacher guides us so that we resolve the conflict ourselves.